GIRL YOU GOT

GOOD VIBES ONLY

GIRLS JUST WANNA HAVE FUNDAMENTAL HUMAN RIGHTS

AMAZING

EMPOWERED WOMEN MAKING AN IMPACT

I AM CHAR GE OF MY LIFE

WELL BEHAVED WOMEN RARELY MAKE HISTORY.

Actually, I CAN!

RIGHTS ARE HUMAN RIGHTS

Achieve Your Goals & Dreams!
Vision Board Clip Art Book

DON'T

~have~ ATTITUDES

MATTER

STRONG WOMEN ARE SHAPING HISTORY

I'M SORRY FOR WHAT I SAID WHEN I WAS HUNGRY

Power

Wellness
Odyssey

Why should I create a Vision Board?

A vision board is a collection of images and words that represent your dreams, wishes, aspirations and goals. Its purpose is to serve as inspiration or motivation. Vision boards use the process and power of visualization - the act or process of interpreting in visual terms the mental images or ideas of what you want to achieve, accomplish or do.

A vision board can be made on anything – a bulletin board, a whiteboard, notebook, scrapbook, tablet, computer screen, or your refrigerator door. It is meant to give you a physical or digital surface to create and arrange the graphics, images, words or phrases that represent what you would like to be, see, achieve or do.

The choice of subject matter, focus or topic is yours – It can be about your work, family, play, travel, fitness or any combination or focus. Let your board represent your immediate goals or your dreams for the future. It's your board, your choice and your direction.

How to create your Vision Board

It's simple! Pick the surface area that you want to use. Make it small, large, attractive or utilitarian. Again, the choice is yours but you probably want it in a spot that will allow you to easily see the images, graphics, and words that represent what you envision. Collect your images, quotes, sayings, words, photos, ticket stubs, memorabilia or anything that inspires you and that represent your goals, dreams and the pathway(s) that you want to follow. Grab some scissors, glue and pushpins and start mapping out your present and future.

Why should I create a Vision Board?

A vision board is a collection of images and words that represent your dreams, wishes, aspirations and goals. Its purpose is to serve as inspiration or motivation. Vision boards use the process and power of visualization - the act or process of interpreting in visual terms the mental images or ideas of what you want to achieve, accomplish or do.

A vision board can be made on anything – a bulletin board, a whiteboard, notebook, scrapbook, tablet, computer screen, or your refrigerator door. It is meant to give you a physical or digital surface to create and arrange the graphics, images, words or phrases that represent what you would like to be, see, achieve or do.

The choice of subject matter, focus or topic is yours – It can be about your work, family, play, travel, fitness or any combination or focus. Let your board represent your immediate goals or your dreams for the future. It's your board, your choice and your direction.

How to create your Vision Board

It's simple! Pick the surface area that you want to use. Make it small, large, attractive or utilitarian. Again, the choice is yours but you probably want it in a spot that will allow you to easily see the images, graphics, and words that represent what you envision. Collect your images, quotes, sayings, words, photos, ticket stubs, memorabilia or anything that inspires you and that represent your goals, dreams and the pathway(s) that you want to follow. Grab some scissors, glue and pushpins and start mapping out your present and future.

GIRL YOU GOT THIS

SHUT THE FRONT DOOR

STRONG WOMEN ARE SHAPING HISTORY

I AM IMPORTANT

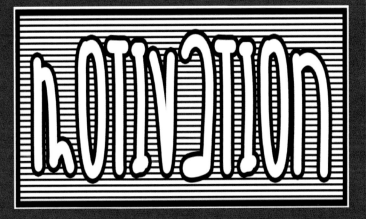

MOTIVATION

genuine

PARTNER

Actually, I CAN!

YOU ARE
SUPER DUPER
AMAZING
TALENTED
GO GETTER
LET NOTHING
STAND IN
YOUR WAY
EVER

happy days

DO
GOOD
DEEDS

STRONG
women
DON'T
have
ATTITUDES

I CAN DO ANYTHING.

DEFINE MY GOALS

She has fire in her SOUL AND grace in her heart

WOMEN'S RIGHTS ♀ ARE ♡ HUMAN RIGHTS

SHE BELIEVED SHE COULD SO SHE DID

NO TIME TO SLEEP

COURAGE

I CHOOSE TO THINK POSITIVELY.

feelin' BADASS

HAPPINESS IS A CHOICE

Month: _____

Key: ☆   ☆   ☆   ☆   ☆   ☆

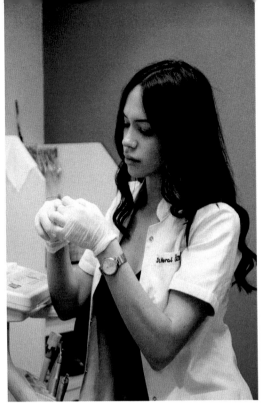

NOTHING IS IMPOSSIBLE

THANKFUL FOR YOU

FUN

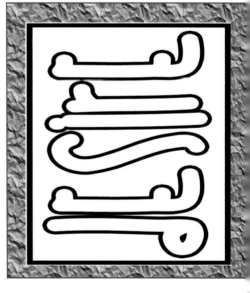

INVESTMENT

MANIFESTATION

I AM IN CHARGE OF MY LIFE

COFFEE:

The power behind entrepreneurship

BEHIND EVERY SUCCESSFUL WOMAN IS *Herself*

- CRAP -
HAPPENS

STRONG WOMEN

RAISE
Strong Girls

Sometimes All That Matters is that you're Still Trying

Bull Crap

you are nice

WELL BEHAVED WOMEN
RARELY MAKE HISTORY.

I MATTER

A yawn is just a silent scream for coffee.

INTELLIGENT *strong* **and** AMAZING

NOW

YOU'RE GONNA BE OKAY

I AM AN AMAZING PERSON.

MEN SHOULDN'T BE MAKING LAWS ABOUT WOMEN'S BODIES

Never UNDERESTIMATE The Power

Underestimate Me That Will Be Fun

MY CONFIDENCE GROWS WHEN I STEP OUTSIDE OF MY COMFORT ZONE.

MY VOICE MATTERS.

EMPOWERED

Shit Happens!

TRUTH
BELIEVE
HOPE

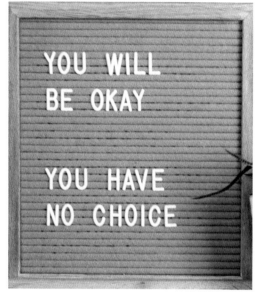

YOU WILL
BE OKAY

YOU HAVE
NO CHOICE

HAPPINESS

I BELIEVE IN MYSELF AND MY ABILITIES.

MEN OF QUALITY RESPECT WOMENS EQUALITY

WHATEVER YOU DO DO IT WELL

GIRL BOSS

I CAN BE ANYTHING I WANT TO BE.

I make my dreams a reality

YOU ARE WORTHY OF LOVE

Charity

MAKE ART

OBEY

NOT WAR

EVERY DAY MAY NOT BE GOOD... BUT THERE IS SOMETHING GOOD IN EVERY DAY.

WISDOM

you GOT THIS

we often take for granted the very things that deserve

our gratitude.

BE THANKFUL

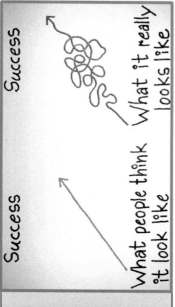

Success

Success

What it really looks like

What people think it look like

Something is better coming

FACT:

IN THE 1800's physicians commonly advised their lovelorn patients to eat chocolate to calm their pining...

ITALIAN
SAUSAGE
+
Peppers
+
Onions

SPECIAL
Chicken
Tenders
WITH
FreshCut
FRENCH
* FRIES *

NOURISHMENT

CLAMS
BEER
SOFT ICE SOFT
CREAM

today is the Perfect day to be happy!

REAL ESTATE

THE FUTURE IS FEMALE

Girl power

Power

HOPE
ALWAYS

YOU ARE
WHAT YOU EAT.
SO DON'T BE:

FAST
CHEAP
EASY
FAKE

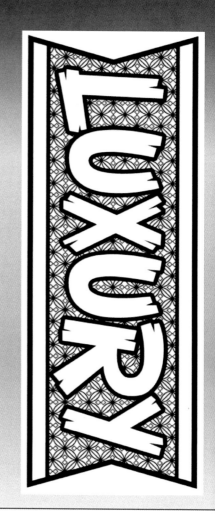

LUXURY

&

STRIVE FOR GREATNESS

SAVINGS

LADY BOSS

ALCOHOL!
it's not the
answer, BUT
makes you forget
the QUESTION

Go up and never stop

CHILDREN
LEFT
UNATTENDED
WILL BE
TOWED AWAY
AT
OWNER'S
EXPENSE

GIRLS JUST WANNA HAVE FUNDAMENTAL HUMAN RIGHTS

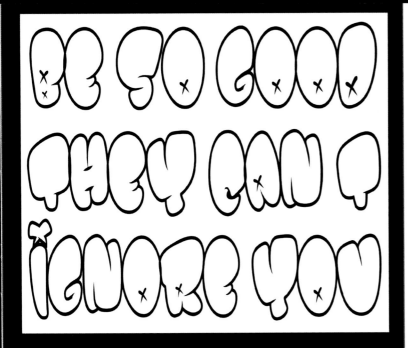

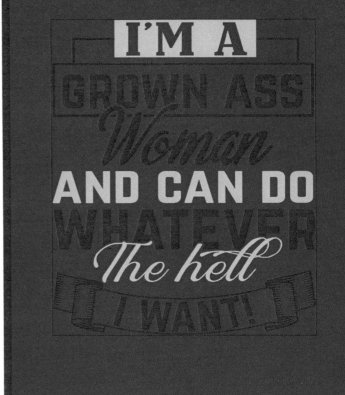

EMPOWERED GIRLS
EMPOWER GIRLS

EMPOWERED WOMEN

EMPOWER WOMEN

0 1 2 3 4 5 6 7 8 9 !

Aa a Bb b Cc c Dd d

Ee e Ff f Gg g Hh h

Ii i i Jj j Kk k Ll l l

Mm m Nn n Oo o Pp p

Qq Rr r r Ss s s

Tt t t Uu Vv Ww ?

Xx Yy Zz . 10

SKILLSET

CLEVER

MORTGAGE

free

believe in yourself

I WILL SEE YOUR
SARCASM

AND RAISE YOU
SOME SASS

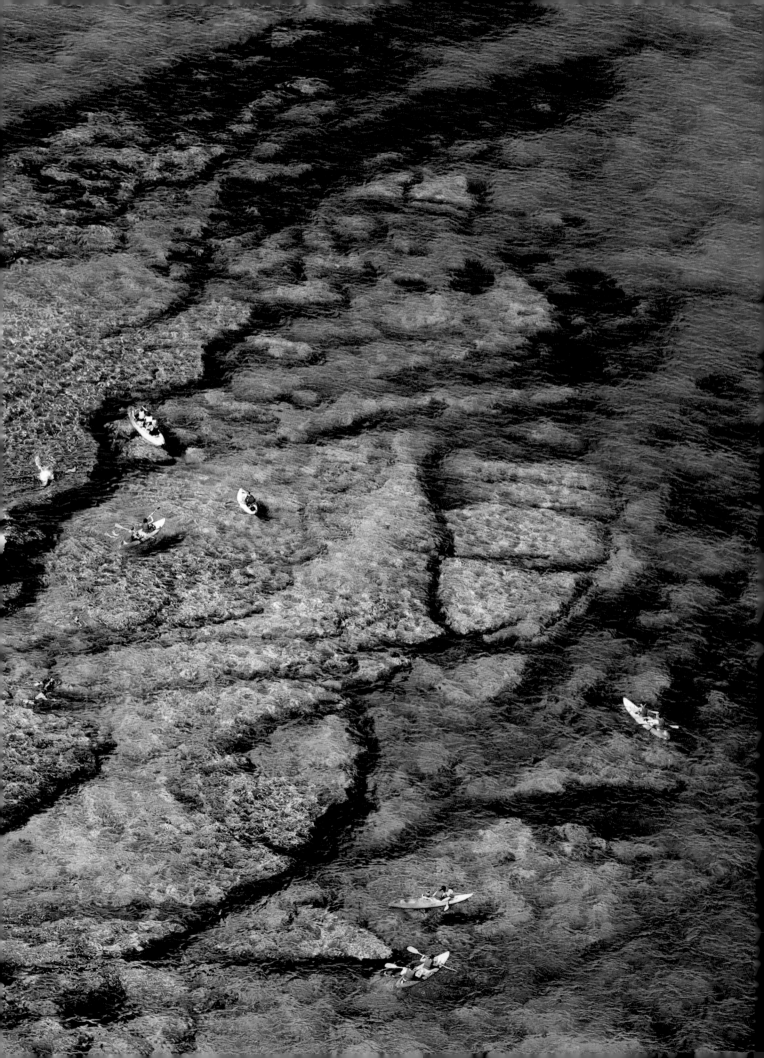

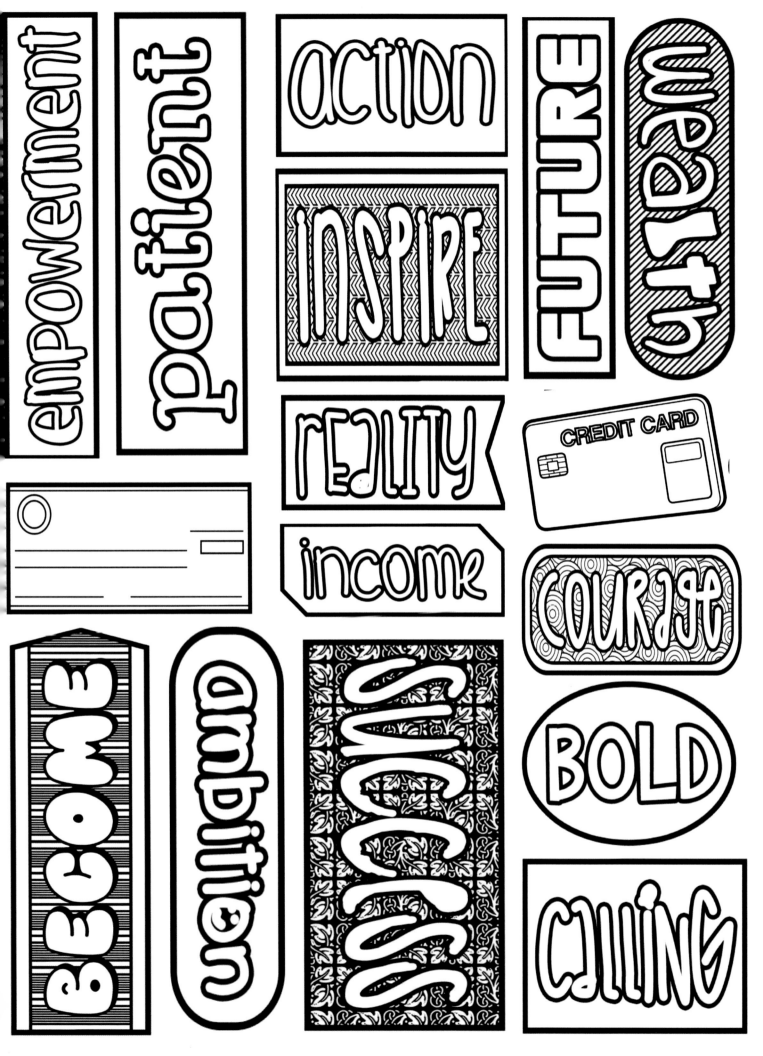

It's okay to fall apart sometimes. Tacos fall apart and we still love them!

LIFE IS SHORT. EAT DESSERT FIRST!

EVERYTHING IS GOING TO BE ALRIGHT

I AM ENOUGH

GRATITUDE

I accept who I am

MEN & WOMEN HAVE EQUAL REWARDS FOR THEIR DEEDS

I'M SORRY FOR WHAT I SAID WHEN I WAS HUNGRY

I AM A WOMAN ON A MISSION TO...

TO MAKE SOMETHING SPECIAL YOU JUST HAVE TO BELIEVE IT'S SPECIAL

THIS WAY FOR LOAN APPROVAL →

Nothing brings people together like good Food! Have a Nice Day!

I START WITH A positive mindset

감사합니다 Natick
Danke Ευχαριστίες Dalu
Grazie Thank You Köszönöm Obrigado
Tack
Спасибо Dank Gracias
谢谢 Merci Seé
ありがとう

BRAINSTORMING
Believe

LIKE
·A·
BOSS

BEAUTIFUL

BADASS

BEAUTY AND BRAINS

MISCHIEVOUS

empowerment

Empowered WOMEN SUPPORT Empowered WOMEN

MENTAL CIRCUMSTANCES PRESEN CAMPAIGNS STRUCTURES EMPHASIZED
AFFIRMATIONS THINKING BRAIN ATTITUDES THOUGHT
ITIVE POSITIVE HEALTH
ATTITUDE POLITICAL EMO
CHANGE IDEA ONE
RMATION

CHARISMA

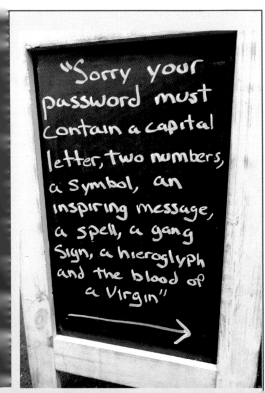

"Sorry your password must contain a capital letter, two numbers, a symbol, an inspiring message, a spell, a gang sign, a hieroglyph and the blood of a virgin"

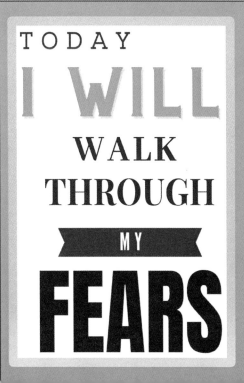

TODAY
I WILL
WALK
THROUGH
MY
FEARS

EVERY CLOUD HAS A SILVER LINING